Our Heaven Baby

by Leah Vis • illustrated by Aeron Brown

THREE HORSE
PUBLISHING

ISBN 978-1-7328118-0-5

To Abel, Roni, Cedar Lily, Glory,
and our three Heaven babies

— Leah

To my child who went to Heaven before we could
meet him, Johnathan David Brown

— Aeron

Hi! My name is Abel, and I'm five years old.
I have a mommy, daddy, and a little sister named Roni.
She's three. We also have a brother.

But, I have a surprise about him. You'll never guess it.
He's in Heaven! Yes, the real Heaven with Jesus and all the angels.
Can you believe it? Let me tell you the story
about our special baby.

One day, my whole family was driving in the car,
and my mommy turned around with smiling eyes.
I just knew she had a secret she couldn't wait to tell us.

"Mommy has a baby in her belly! We're going to have our
very own baby, and it's a little boy!" she said.

Whoa! Roni and I were so excited. We started asking all sorts
of questions. My heart felt like it was doing bunny hops.
I was so happy!

We even went with Mommy to one of her check-ups,
and we heard the tiny ba-boom, ba-boom,
ba-boom of our brother's heart.

I couldn't see the baby in Mommy's tummy, but I could
hear him in there. And I just couldn't stop smiling.

Mommy must have been excited too.
Whenever she talked about the baby, it was like
she was singing. I felt like singing too . . . and dancing,
and hopping, and flipping!

I couldn't wait to hold my brother and teach him
how to be a kid.

And then one day, when Roni and I were playing together,
Mommy and Daddy said they wanted to talk to us.
Mommy's eyes were a little shiny, and she didn't have the
song in her voice. She said, "Our baby has died and is now
in Heaven with Jesus."

Hmmmm, that's weird. Mommy and Daddy talked
some more, but I kinda forgot to listen. I did hear
one thing, though—Heaven. Heaven?

"Really, Mommy? Heaven?" I had never known anyone
to go to Heaven before. My very own baby brother is in Heaven?

My mommy said, "Let's dream about what it's like.
I bet our baby loves it there!"

I started to imagine it. When we go to Heaven, will we walk
on the clouds? Or maybe they're so fluffy that it's more like bouncing.
I hope we can get our noses really close to a rainbow. I'm just sure
rainbows smell like summer berries.

"Daddy, what about Goldie, Roger, Mr. Whiskers, and Bunny Bun?
Do you think we'll see all our pets in Heaven?" I asked.
Daddy said that whatever we love here, well,
Heaven will be even better.

"Mommy, are there lots of kids to play with?"

"Yes, love. I'm sure there are tons of kids there who love to play.

What do you think they do for fun?"

Dreaming about Heaven was so fun! I thought that maybe each kid might have a dinosaur to play with.

And I giggled about how silly it would be to surprise Jesus from behind. I would grab his hands, and we would swing around and sing until we fall on the ground laughing.

I wonder if anyone ever stops smiling in Heaven. I bet they
can if they want. But then they would see an angel flying,
or Jesus dancing, and that smile would come right back.
I think I would laugh a lot.

In Heaven, I think everyone's hearts are bursting
with happy songs—like Mommy's did when the baby
was in her tummy.

We talked so much about Heaven that I had to jump up
and walk around silly. Heaven is going to be so much fun!

And then we laughed and hugged because our very own brother
is in Heaven. "Mommy, we're going to have a big family
in Heaven!"

I know I won't get to see my brother until
I go to Heaven, but then we'll play
together forever.

I think I can wait for that.

About the Author

Leah Vis

Leah is a mother to four kids on Earth and three kids in Heaven. As this story tells, Leah and her husband, Rob, had two kids and then experienced three consecutive miscarriages. After that they were able to have two more kids, so yes, their family will be very big in Heaven.

Leah is an author, speaker, and relentless encourager. She writes from a childlike and wonder-full perspective. And she speaks on miscarriage, finding breakthrough, healing, hearing God, parenting, hope, and everything in between.

To hear more of Leah's story or invite her to speak at your next event, visit www.leahvisauthor.com.

About the Illustrator

Aeron Brown

Aeron Razz Brown was born and raised in the Inland Empire of Southern California. When Aeron was very young, his father passed away. As any son would, Aeron wanted to connect with his father through the very few ways he knew how: art and music. Aeron immersed himself in his father's sketches, lyrics, and creativity. He started collaging his father's scraps of artwork into his drawings and later on started collecting vintage, found objects onto his own hand-painted works of art.

Aeron captures light and beauty with a modern indie style of acrylic painting. He shares his vibrant, colorful creations all over Southern California.

To see more of Aeron's artwork, visit www.aeronbrown.com.